"Unapologetic"

More Lyrical Thought
of a
St. Louis Poet

by Cynthia Walker

Copyright 2022 by Granny's Goodies and Giftables

All rights reserved, including the right to reproduce this book or portions there of in any form whatsoever. Including photocopying, recording, or by any information storage and retrieval system, without permission in writing from the copyright owner.

ISBN-13: 979-8-9850205-1-9

Printed in the USA

PUBLISHED BY: Granny's Goodies and Giftables
COVER ART: Cynthia Walker
COVER LAYOUT: LJ Thomas

CONTACT INFO:
IG: LyricalThoughtStLPoet
Podcast: Lyrical Thoughts Of A St Louis Poet on several platforms.
FB: Lyrical Thoughts Of A St. Louis Poet
To order signed copies… email…
LyricalthoughtsStLPoet@gmail.com

Dedication

I have decided to dedicate this, my collection of unapologetically thought provoking, emotion evoking poetry, to… Tink…

Tink is the nickname given to me by my father. He passed away when I was very young. My Aunt Gina occasionally reminds me how I would announce my name proudly to all who asked… Cynthia Denise Jones, Tink Tink. Over the years as I got older it became just Tink, and I know if I hear it now, it's a friend or family member who's calling me.

After my husband passed, I found that I had to rediscover myself as an individual. I had been for the last 31 years a stepmom, grandmother, and wife. I had to remind myself who Tink was before becoming part of the family unit. As I venture down this path of self-re-discovery. Tink is living my life like its golden, and it is again to Tink, that I dedicate this book.

Now with that being said…

There are so very many people who have contributed to the reality of this book.
There are those who endured my constant poetic references to… everything… all the time lol.
Those who have been there to read and offer honest opinions about my work. And those who are the encouraging voices that remind me that I *should* share my poetic thoughts, because words are powerful. And I dedicate all I do to God, above all others. To each of you, I say thank you for… Encouraging, Appreciating, Tolerating and Loving me. You are all appreciated. I don't feel a need to try to name everyone. I give thanks and show appreciation all the time, so you know who you are. Thank You and I love you each, unapologetically.

Introduction

Hi again, I'm back to share more of my poetry. Friends and family tell me that the message needs to be heard. So, in this collection, I'd like to introduce you to a different side of Lyrical Thoughts, the St Louis Poet. My first book reflected the poetry written to give praise, and uplift, in times of trials and tribulations. During my first cancer battle, it was suggested that I keep a journal. It began as a Dear God letter writing book, but as I wrote more, I found that I could work through my emotions with poetry. I published the collection "Inspired" Lyrical Thoughts Of A St Louis Poet, in hopes that the words written that helped me, would help others in difficult times as well.

In this collection, I unapologetically share thought provoking poetic thoughts and opinions on a much larger variety of subjects. I share how I feel about subjects that other choose not to talk about. Poetry conveys emotions and perspective on even touchy subjects like domestic violence, abortion, paternity drama, and senseless violence. I even have included my small collection of erotic poetry as a last chapter for ADULTS ONLY. Poetry is a reflection of thoughts and opinions. It is used to evoke emotion or thought. In many cases, real life situations and occurrences inspire poets to write. I chose the title "Unapologetic" to serve as a disclaimer to the reader. These are my opinions expressed and although our opinions and/or outlooks may be different, I hope you, nevertheless, enjoy the poetic flow of my… Lyrical Thoughts.

Table of Contents

My Hood	11
Birds Of A Feather	13
Opioid Crisis Victim VS Heroin Addict	14
Don't Judge A Book By It's Cover	15
Karen	16
Strike One! You're Out!	17
Creativity Without Content	18
Kingdom Crowns	19
Bombarded With Negativity	21
Brothas	23
Crazy	25
Bad Vibes	27
Hey MOMMA!	29
Cell Phones And Unlimited Access	31
New Norm	33
Proclamation 95	35
Red Bottoms	37
Thug Life Regrets	39
Mommy's Boyfriend's Wife	41
Your Guilty Conscience	43
New Day	44
Patience Without Purpose	45
You Don't Need To Tell Me Your Truth	46
Young Angry Black Man	47
Reckless	48
Niggas…	49
Who's This Dude In Charge	50

Valued	53
Call It Like It Is	54
Perjurer	56
Ain't Nothin' Weak 'Bout Being Christian	58
Love Is Pain	59
Silence Is A Mighty Tool	61
Another Lesson, Another Loss	62
There Is Always Something Just Out Of View	63
Let Go	65
Bored In The House	67
Happy, Happy, Merry Day	69
So Much Advice	70
Melting Pot	71
Sorry Jerry Springer	72
Tune Out Game	73
Ali	75
Bottom Of The Totem Pole	76
Butch	77
Why Not?	79
Survivor	80
Shocking Discoveries	81
End Game	84
Ashamed	85
Thanks For Letting Me Be Part Of Your Struggle	86
Tell Me	88
This Is My Square	89
Damn Mama	90
Respect	92
I Can't Breathe	94

Zero Motive	96

Poems to come and ones missed:

Poems that can be found in the upcoming book "Fractured Folks", A St Louis Poet's Lyrical Thoughts On The Human Condition

My 2 Me's	97
Teach One	98
The Love Meant For Me	100
Adoptee	101

Poems you missed if you haven't read my first book "Inspired" Lyrical Thoughts of A St Louis Poet

What's the All	104
One	105
Vessel	107

As mentioned in the Introduction. Many things inspire poets to write. Erotic poetry is a genre that I have only dabbled in. I have a small collection of erotic poetry and I've decided, where else, but in "Unapologetic" would I be appropriately, inappropriate.

So… be warned, if you don't like dirty words or thoughts, you'll want to avoid these.

Hood Chicks	110
Wet Words Wednesday	112
BDC	114
Stranger Danger	116

My Hood

Lots and lots of unfamiliarity
As I travel along very familiar roads
Many changes, meshed with history
Oh my, how "My Hood" has grown

Years of standing in the shadows
Of all we viewed was good
I had a determination, and burning desire
To expand my experience beyond "My Hood"

Belief of a good life just 'cross the Mississippi
Opportunity, nightlife, glitz and glam
A stark opposite of my hood, "Shanty"
It won't be, what defines, who I am

I took a moment to visit my old hood
And found so many, many things have changed
Oh Snap, is that Ms. Ellie, still sitting on the corner
And suddenly "My Hood" feels just the same

My hood still lies in the shadows
Some have ventured back to ensure change
But it's a never ending, uphill battle
Deep rooted Hood mentality remains

Thank you "My Hood" for the memories
Some good, some educational, and some just bad
But I'll cherish all the varied experiences
Cause they chronicle the life that I've had

I am a stronger, and smarter person
A culmination of where I've been
Learning lessons from ALL my actions
"My Hood" is my history… It's where my life began

Birds Of A Feather

Birds of a feather, flock together
Ever seen a duck fly with crows?
Birds of a feather flock together
That's simply how it goes

If you don't want to be judged by the flock?
Then chart your own flight path
Don't believe and react to situations
Just cause "That's what Ray Ray and them said"!

Choose to be your own man
Stand tall on your own two feet
Don't fall victim to the temptation
That you WILL, encounter in the streets

Make your own life's decisions
Suffer only your own, consequence
And when "'crazy" comes your way
"RIGHT" will be your best defense

Be your own man with your head held high,
When all in life around you, wants to go low,
Revolt and put Your best foot forward
And your brilliant, individuality will show

Opioid Crisis Victim VS Heroin Addict

Opioid crisis victim vs heroin addict
How can you separate the two?
Let's see, one of them lives on Crenshaw
And the other? Well, she lives with You

How dare you! MY kid's no criminal
She only stole money and drugs from Me
She took Percocet from my pocketbook
Those are prescription drugs, you see

Now the drugs are no longer, just in the hood
Now that it's affecting other classes
We file lawsuits against the drug dealers
Called class action, and they're filed by the masses

Opioid crisis victim vs heroin addict
How can you separate the two?
Well one of them lives in Compton
And the other? She lives with You

Don't Judge A Book By Its Cover

Please don't judge this book by its cover
As interesting as the cover art may be
You'll be delighted, intrigued and maybe inspired
If you choose to continue to read

So please don't judge a book by its cover
You could miss adventure, or opportunities
Don't be quick to judge books by their covers
Who knows, it may be a great story indeed

Karen

Who the hell do you think you are?
What makes you the boss of "everything"?
Never seeing a need to apologize
Why are you so rude and mean?

I won't listen to your pretentious talk
You ain't no F N better than me
What makes you so damn arrogant
What a jaded reality you see

Confidence is one thing
But your image of you, leans to the left
You look through rose-colored glasses
When you're looking at yourself.

Who the hell do you think you are?
What makes you the boss of "Everything"
Be aware you should stop running up on "Folks"
Before "Folks" opt to bring you to your knees.

Get over yourself, and learn to chill
Check that "at-ti-tude" at your own front door
And learn to just chill and behave in public
And life will offer you so much more

Strike 1! You're OUT!

Strike 1! You're OUT! Fuck 2 and 3.
Why give a liar a second chance?
If I can't trust or believe what I'm hearing
Keep your fake ass love, and romance

Respect is gone, loyalty null and void
Love and adoration have dissipated
Your moral reputation has been lost
Thank God, I've been extricated

Your hustle and grind, lack integrity
You care not who you use, or hurt
Taking advantage of other's weaknesses
Leaving victims, lying in the dirt

Strike 1! You're OUT! Fuck 2 and 3.
Why give a liar a second chance?
Can't trust or believe what I'm hearing
Keep your fake ass love, and romance

Creativity Without Content

Creativity without content
Is an empty copy of all the rest
Creativity with heart and passion
Shines undisputedly, as the best

Dreams without imaginative foundation
Are pretty pictures stored in your mind
Fueling the chasing of someone else's dreams
And not one of your own design

What is the basis of your passion?
Creativity, Money, or Fame?
All that glitters is not gold my friend
Your choice, could bring a crazy game

Life has a way of working out, as it should
Some things happen for reasons quite unknown
Then other times, the harvest that you find you're reaping
Is exactly what has been sown

Creativity without content
Is an empty copy of all the rest
Creativity with heart and passion
Shines undisputedly, as the best

Kingdom Crowns

Errbody wanna be top of the heap
Kings, Queens, Gods, and Goddesses alike
But are you down for your kingdom's subjects?
Do you take responsibility for easing kingdom strife?

Royalty and divinity, both come with responsibility
Are you qualified to be God/Goddess, King or Queen?
Or did you just decide to adopt a title?
Cause now a days, that seems to be a thing

Now it's all pretty simple, in my opinion
Some of us must be happy to be support
Realizing that many roles make up a successful kingdom
I'm content to effectively, and loyally do my part

My happiness or status, is not defined by others opinion
My behavior is proof positive of my worth
I am, my best me and with that, I am delighted
I simply have no need, to strive to be first

Err body wanna be the G.O.A.T.
Always striving to surpass… "Who's next?"
Yet life's delights lie in the satisfaction
And pride in knowing, you've done your best

We all have a role in the betterment of humanity
And hierarchy in life's pecking order is not claimed, but earned
Kingdoms come with adoring, loyal subjects
With, whose best interest, the crown, must be concerned

So, when you decide to claim royal or divine status
Be aware that, heavy is the head that wears the crown
And understand that King/Queen,
God/Goddess,
Are words of action, not just nouns

Bombarded With Negativity

Bombarded with negativity
Inundated with more bad news
Intently watching the world's sad, goings ons
Bringing the masses to sing the blues

Each, and every, single day
There are more tales, of man gone awry
Guns and drugs in every household
The perfect recipe for someone to die

We profess to be so progressive
Fair and just, in our judgment of... "everything"
But take a look at truth, and the sad reality
Equality is hella far from... Dr. King's dream

If you put garbage in, you'll get garbage out
Please don't try to expect anything else
Don't blindly follow the path of others
Make your decisions for yourself!

You'll be bombarded with more negativity
But despite the more bad news
Keep YOUR head up and outlook positive
Bring a brightness when you enter any room

Some walk and talk what they believe in
Like LeBron James, Kaepernick, Lupe and Misty C.
Showing that having conviction does pay off
Sharing that very part of you, encouraging every successful me

Seek out something better
You're not chained to your past
Don't insanely keep doing the same thing
While expecting a different outcome, from the last

With one, and one, and several one mores
We CAN implement a positive change
We CAN teach each other, tolerance
So we are all turning to the same page

Brothas

A Brotha can't hide his identity
There's no question that he's black
No education, employment, or status
Has, or will ever, change that fact

Stevie Wonder said it best, to us
"You may have the cash, but you can't cash in that face"
Black men are perceived as bad men
Based solely on their race

Each day as he leaves his home
His reality draws a very thin line
If perception says he's crossed it
Without provocation, death may be the fine

Routine becomes extreme quickly
When a black man is involved
Encounters strained and violent
That otherwise could have been peacefully resolved

Not all brothas are criminals
Who are worthy of guns being drawn
Officer? I simply failed to signal
This inhumane treatment is just wrong

Too many black men shot and killed
By those who vowed to protect and serve
Community and law can't live harmoniously
When justice lines, are so horribly blurred

A Brotha can't hide his identity
There's no question that he's black
No education, employment, or status
Has, or will ever, change that fact

Crazy

This shit is just fucking crazy
7 year old's can't play in their own backyard
Because cowards and worthless criminals
Drive by, shooting children from their cars

Too many innocent children are being buried
Please don't tell me how the good die young
Damn man, Really? Nobody saw nothin'?
Our passivity show that evil has already won

We stay fully engaged with our social media
Complaining 'bout dumb shit, we seek out to dislike
While Damn Man, Really? Nobody saw nothing
As another of our babies loses his life

I heard a man suggest a 'lil hood justice
Find those responsible and kick that ass
Reclaim our own lives, and neighborhoods
Cause its current condition is just sad

We must take responsibility for our own village
And the villagers may need to take up arms
And let these worthless invaders know simply
We won't allow you to do more children harm

Heavy hearted are the parents and families
That have experienced a senseless, tragic loss
No one else is gonna fix this problem for us
We must join and rise against this evil force

Afraid to turn on the news in the morning
Sick from learning another child has died
Damn man, Really? Nobody saw nothing
Fear in the air is making too many blind

It's time to join together without fear
Let these killers know, ENOUGH!... NO MORE!
All eyes and cross hairs are locked on your behavior
We won't accept the same shit as before

Bad Vibes

Bad vibes will affect your well being
Despairing thoughts, bore into your brain
Confrontational bad company, with bad intentions
Coupled with bad words, and your life could, suddenly change

Words, most certainly have power
Many thoughts and emotions can they bring
Folks speak with, and without consideration for others
Often not clearly saying, what they mean

No time in life, for real, for confrontation
But occasionally, avoidance is not a choice
But be warned, I know How To Go There Wit Cha!
YOU WILL NOT SILENCE MY OPINION, OR MY VOICE!

Not happy with who you've encountered?
You've lots of suggestions on what to improve
Sorry to make you aware so harshly
I have no interest, in an opinion... from you

So "Back Up" Because We ain't even Potna's
And "Dat Shit" you did, was just foul
You approached me "Mad Disrespectful"
SMH! REALLY?, WTF?, "WOW"

Bad vibes will affect your well being
Don't let them bring your spirits down
Avoid bad company with bad intentions
Don't keep negativity around

Hey MOMMA!

What was that whizzing past me?
Oh, snap, here come some more
Oh look, there's a very pushy one,
Banging at my outer door

What a feisty little thing he is,
He's forced his way right in
He's now inside my outer shell,
And now, a new life begins

Oh wow, I'm feeling funny,
As things begin to grow
I have a cute little face now,
And things to wiggle down below

I grow bigger as I develop,
I now have a thumb to suck
But I hear my Mommy crying,
Doesn't she see me as good enough?

Hey, what's that? What are they doing?
What is that little light?
What have they sent in here with me?
It's cold and doesn't feel right

Oh Mommy, what's that awful noise?
Why won't they let me be?
They seem to be trying to force me out,
Oh Lord, is she getting rid of me?

Why Mommy, What did I do wrong,
Aren't I special enough for you?
You didn't even give me the chance,
To show you what I could do

Oh no! Here comes that thing again,
This time it's pulling harder
It seems today's my final day,
I won't get to grow into your beautiful daughter

Mommy, why did you end my life?
Why wasn't I meant to be
How will you handle, Mommy?
The memory, of the death, of me

Cell Phones And Unlimited Access

Cell phones, Wi-Fi, and unlimited access...
Instantaneous world interaction on a whim
Placed in the hands of the irresponsible
Is how rumors and dangerous challenges begin

Causing far rippling effects and action,
With no logical thought required
Potential consequence caused for many, instantly
With no regard or regret for... content, nor intent desired

No other object, has been launched, with such success
Inundating the masses so complete and without exclusivity
Controlling households, finance of and communication for
Man/Woman, Young/Old, Rich/Poor, All dependent on, connectivity

Yeah, me too, I'm hooked, like everyone else
I will go back, if I find I've left my phone
Later realizing, I simply didn't need it
And in fact, could have left it at home

Folks are living life through a cell phone
Living online comes with a hefty price
Missing," Once in a lifetime experiences" ...
As you're trolling, liking, or ranting, late at night

Cell phones and unlimited access, and... world interaction on a whim
With no logical thought required
Causing consequence and effect for many, instantly
 With no regard or regret for... content, nor the intent desired

New Norm

Panic, has never inspired solution
Fear never leads to a positive end
Prayer, however, is very powerful
It's where resolutions often begin

Life is now filled with uncertainty
A new norm must now be found
Be more responsible for your surroundings
And more selective of who you're around

There are lessons to learn via COVID
Like, who cares about their fellow man?
And who's not taking this very seriously
And who selfishly bucks solution's collective plan

Lives are now filled with uncertainty
A new world norm must be found
Be more responsible for your behavior
And more selective of who you're around

Remember when the panic is over
All the who's and how's and the why's
Remember who just had to, "turn-up"
While the WORLD was staying inside

Lives now filled with uncertainty
New routines now must be found
Keeping close, only treasured loved ones
Being selective of who you're around

Proclamation 95

Proclamation 95 gave slaves emancipation
And was signed by Abe Lincoln, September 1862
However, its enactment was not to be immediate
101 more days of slavery, before freedom, would be true (Jan 1863)

Three million plus, Blacks were
granted freedom
Objective? Save the Union, Not Human Care
250,000 Slaves in border states were excluded
900 more days, they'd endure agony and despair
(June 1865)

When finally, the last were told that slavery was over
The "Freed" were advised, to stay on as Staff
They were told their idleness would not be tolerated.
But truth was ole Massa needed dem slaves real bad

Praised was Ole Abe when he finally decided
That "Freedom" was more lucrative than not
For it certainly it wasn't bout destroying "Evil Slavery"
Cause Texas enslaved 900 more days. Damn that's a lot!

Proclamation 95, gave slaves emancipation
Yet "Freedom" and "Equality" are both ongoing struggles
You simply can not live Unaffected by Inequality
There's certainly no racist free, "Equality Bubble"

Red Bottoms

Red Bottoms Red Bottoms
Not the kind you may know
Her shoes have red bottoms
From the blood on the floor

Fire Red fingernails
Again, not what you think
Her nails are fire red
From the blood in the sink

She really don't like him
But he pays all the bills
And except for pole twerkin'
She ain't got no skills

He don't like her for real either
He calls her a whore
One day he got angry and beat her
Shed her blood on the floor

She wanted to leave him
But he paid all the bills
He said he'd love her forever
But his love wasn't real

He bought her red bottoms
Got her off the dance floor
Took her home then he caged her
And beat her worse than before

One day she grew tired
Chose to not take anymore
Now her shoes have red bottoms
And he lays lifeless on the floor

Red bottoms, Red bottoms
Not the kind you may know
Her shoes have red bottoms
From his blood on the floor

Thug Life Regrets

WTF did I do the other night
I think I fucked up and shot and killed a kid
And although I don't think that anyone saw me do it
God, and I, know exactly what I did

This thuggin' shit is all I've ever known
It's all I've ever seen, or ever been taught
But now, ain't a soul or dollar that can save me
I'll pay the price for the consequence my actions bought

May as well tell you how this shit happened
Ole boy disrespected me a week or so ago in the club one night
And, I didn't have my piece on me because of security
But I told that nigga to be ready for a fight

Then just the other day I saw him parked on the corner
Not paying attention, he was looking for something in the back seat
I thought to myself, Yeah smart mouth, now I got you
It was the perfect opportunity for me

I stepped quickly and deliberately straight towards him
Pulled out my piece and bullets started to spray
Then I heard the scream of a child crying out for daddy
My life changed and theirs were lost on that day

WTF did I do the other night
I fucked up, I shot and killed a kid
And although I don't think anyone saw me do it
God and I, know exactly, what I did

Mommy's Boyfriend's Wife

My mother's, boyfriends, wife,
Can't stand the sight of me
Daddy has been her husband 5 years
And I am only 3

Mommy's oldest, my big sis, is turning 8
But, he's not her daddy too
Just me and my little brother
He's the wife's child, and he's 2

Now Mommy is getting mad a lot
Always yelling at my dad
She says he can't come back again
I'm feeling super sad

She says I'm just too little
And one day I'll understand
But all that I can tell you
Is that, I really miss my dad

The last time that I saw him
He said he would stay in touch
But when he calls, she won't answer
Oh God, it's all too much

I'm feeling sad and lonely
Gonna try what was on that tv show
I chewed up all of Mommy's nasty pills
Now I lie lifeless, on the floor

Your Guilty Conscience

I won't try to resolve your guilty conscience
Gotta handle that on your own
When the subject hits close and personal
You become rude and belligerent on the phone

We can't seem to disagree peacefully
You seem to always think you're right
When unsolicited advice is rejected
You wanna get loud and start a fight

My arguing days are far behind
Can't impose your guilt on me
And if mean shit is all you have to offer
Gone, is where I need to be

New Day

Although he died in my arms
I offered condolences to you
Extended bushels of olive branches
Don't know what else a Sista can do

I must find a way to go on
My loss really more than you care to know
But also, bout my strength, you're confused
Gonna excel, just watch me grow

I made many promises
And I managed to keep them all
For that I hold my head high
Stepping forward, shoulders back, standing tall

If you ain't bringing good tidings
Keep yo drama to yourself
Decide If you can handle being potnas
Cause there just ain't nothing else

There's a new day on the horizon
Trying hard to learn lots that's new
Wanna experience life like it's my last day
Cause tomorrow ain't promised to you.

Patience Without Purpose

Patience without purpose is procrastination
Delaying the inevitable, but eventual outcome
While wasting time wishing things were different
When the chance of that... is, probably None

So don't fool yourself into thinking
That one plus one, doesn't equal two
For then you alone, will be responsible for your disappointment
There will be no one to blame for your sorrow, but you

Trust and Believe, there's a blessing out there for you
And it will be... Right on Time, like all blessings before
So, get ready, stay ready, and strive to be worthy
To reap the fruits of what God has in store

Patience without purpose is simple, procrastination
Delay of an inevitable, but certain outcome
But patience, with God's purpose in mind is rewarding
And risk of disappointment, is None

You Don't Need To Tell Me Your Truth

You don't need to tell ME your truth
But be honest with yourself
You don't have to confess to others
It's you, and God that matters, No One Else

Don't be your own worst enemy
Trying to lie and reinvent the truth
Bout shit you've done in your adulthood
And some shit done to you in your youth

There's always hope for recovery
From anything you've had to endure
First, we must look inward at our own behavior
And be sure we don't repeat the "Before"

No need to tell ME your truth
But please be honest with yourself
Cause your "After" is in your hands
Take the reins for how you feel, Fuck how you felt.

Young Angry Black Man

Young angry black man
Why are you so mad?
Tell us of your struggle
Of the treatment, which makes you sad

You know you're as good as the others
But your journey is oh so hard
And all they can tell you is, Keep your head up
They tell you to stay strong

While all the while they shun you
Make you feel like less than a man
But maybe with some true compassion
They will come to understand

Stand up young man, you're precious
Stand up to life itself
Stand up young man, you're valuable
To life, love and God himself.

Reckless

No care for the consequences
Facing you or that you've caused for others
Earning the nickname, Damn Lucky
Given as a youngster, with warnings, from your mother

You've always been a fearless daredevil
Impulsive with your actions as well as words
Inconsiderate, with your, tongue, too quick to lash out
Misunderstandings bout what you've said, versus what was heard

Recklessness, reaps just what is sown
Thoughtless, careless, actions and exhibitions
Will bring forth, certain, limitless troubles
And a life filled with strife and contradictions

No care for the consequences
Facing you or that you've cause for others
Earning the nickname, Damn Lucky
Given as a youngster, with warnings, from your mother

Niggas...

Niggas are so fuckin' stupid
That's just a fact of life
Always hollerin bout inequality
Harsh reality, self-inflicted strife

Pissed at Kanye, some say, rightfully so
Cause he called slavery, A choice
But didn't many many fight and die for us
So we may express even an ignorant voice?

Hesitant to say niggas are fuckin stupid
Cause many will assume that means blacks
But niggas are niggas are niggas
And color is not what makes them that

Stupidity, ignorance, prejudice, and pride
Come as varied as the rainbow
Being a nigga is not who you are
But what you refuse to know...

Who's in Charge

Donald Drump, Oh My Goodness
What will the man do to us next?
He certainly suffers from affluenza
He's a few cards short of a full deck

What a horrible mistake was made
To put this man in charge
The divide that he has created
Is extremely damaging, and large

He has been in charge for far too long
And life no longer makes any sense
But Please, Let us all say a prayer for him
Things won't be any better with Dence

Power has ruined and crazed Drump
Let's hold this craziness down to four
Come to your senses "The Masses"
Don't repeat the stupidity from before

Now, what you've just read was written years ago
And sadly, it is all still true
But this man has lost his fucking mind
Inject disinfectant? Is what he suggested that we do?

Can't understand why he hasn't been fired
Or at the very least, fired at
And before you wanna come for me
I'm certainly not suggesting that

Hitler, Napoleon, and Caligula
Crazed leaders, this shit is real
This Nut is not the boss of me
On my momma nugga, FRFR

The unemployed asked for a lil help
Drump said, No problem, don't worry I've got your back
Then gave you $1200, to live on for 6/8 months?
Bruh? What I'm s'pose to do with that

Donald Drump, Oh My Goodness
What will the man do to us next?
He belongs in an insane asylum
He's a few cards short of a full deck

What a horrible mistake was made
To put this man in charge
The danger he has created
The death toll? staggeringly large

So please, please? Come next election November?
Suit up, be safe and head on out your door
Take your power to the polls and vote
And correct the mistake, made before

Sometimes we must amend our poetry
Like this one, I just can't keep up
So, in closing I'll just say let's sit back and watch
The downfall and demise of Donald Drump

Valued

Folks out here, going broke, trying to look rich
Please, explain to me how that makes sense
The fakeness you choose to spend, hard earned coins on
Mimic things valued, for show of perceived "influence"

Insecurities inundated those purchases
Of things, given importance, just not real
Leaving... your self-worth contingent
On how the masses, may currently feel

Folks out here, going broke, trying to look rich
Please, explain to me how that makes sense
The fakeness you choose to spend, hard earned coins on
Mimic things valued, for show of perceived "influence"

Instead, stand out as unique and different
Bopping your head to your own heart's beat
Living your best life like it's golden
With no interest in "influence" perceived

Call It Like It Is

We don't wanna call out our own behavior
Hesitant to say, it is what it is
We wouldn't be quick to offer an opinion
If said behavior was ours, and not his

So very quickly we're willing to pass judgment
On how the next man ought to live
Each life journey is quite different
Leading you to your life, and him to his

We won't call out our own behavior
Hesitant to speak the truth of what it is
Slow down the quick harsh judgments
Circumstance could be yours and not his

Perjurer

Perjury, now that's a serious offense
You know It could land yo' ass in jail
Unless your lie is told in paternity court
About to who, you gave, that tail

She'll tell a tale of fidelity
When that's simply not the truth
She'll blame it on failed birth control
And not, it's simple lack of use

How often can you go to court?
To ask, who fathered your child
Before you change YOUR behavior
Stop turnin' up, and acting wild

Don't be that girl with "baby daddies"
Don't be a "Friend with Benefits"
Have self respect and demand better
Than settling for, a "situationship"

Find substance, beyond good lookin'
"He" may be the father of your kid
Don't be mad at me for saying it
Cause that's exactly how it is

Please don't shoot the messenger
The message is loud and clear
Truth is, twins with different fathers
How many times on Maury, have you appeared?

Take some pride in your existence
Find something, productive, to do
And don't put your feet on the ceiling
For all who'll buy dinner for you

Ok, sounds harsh and cruel I know
But behavior becomes worse and worse
Instead…. try using old school values
And let your husband be your first

C'mon ladies, really, how low is it?
Casual sex in the stall in a public restroom
If this continues to be life's new norm?
Morality and decency are forever doomed

So please don't be a perjurer
That can land yo ass in jail
Don't be that chick who lies in paternity court
Bout who you gave some tail

Ain't Nothing Weak Bout Being Christian

Peter too, was a Christian
He was Jesus's Ride or Die
But he would cut an Opp, bout his homeboy
Check the records, I ain't tellin' no lie

See, the 12, were new followers, not angels
They had a past, full of some bad thangs
But then, you see... they ran into Jesus
The man who was spitting, God's Redemption game

Simon, he was a hustling politician
And he brought the same energy, just now to serving the Lord
Then, they straight "kicked it", and threw a big party
When ya boy, "Matt the Tax Collector", came on board

Then there was Judas, a self-proclaimed thief and embezzler
His greed and betrayal, ultimately responsible for Jesus's demise
Potter's Field was "bought" with Christ blood, and the 30 pieces
To bury the poor, near where he died

Psalms says that the meek shall inherit…
Don't mistake meekness for weakness, or fear
Ain't nothing weak 'bout being a Christian
Peter tried to take Malchusi's head, not his ear

Peter too, was absolutely a Christian
He was, FRFR Jesus's Ride or Die
He would cut an Opp, bout his homeboy
Check the records, I ain't tellin' you, no lies

Love Is Pain

Once I heard that love is pain
And I was first inclined to agree
Yet found no pain in my children's eyes
When they lovingly looked at me

We idolize, then call it love
Then we're hurt when it's not reciprocated
True love, without selfish agenda
If found, will leave you elated

The pain that is caused by loss
Is not love, but the lack thereof
Lack of the chance to make new memories
Memories with the ones we have loved

Once I heard that love is pain
And I was first inclined to agree
Yet found no pain in my children's eyes
When they lovingly looked at me

Silence Is A Mighty Tool

Silence is a mighty tool
Don't owe you how I feel
And through my mighty silence
You will learn what's true and real

Wondering just how bad you hurt me?
Thought I would crumble? Maybe even fall?
Must have forgotten, I am a survivor
And now our trust has been dissolved

Silence is a mighty tool
I don't owe you anything
Cause all I've ever brought to you
Is love, that I made the choice to bring

I ain't nobody's daughter or mother
And now, I ain't nobody's wife
And if you ain't bringing good tidings
I don't need you in my life
Silence is a mighty tool
Ain't gotta share my thoughts and dreams
Cause with your telling actions
You've shown me what my love means

I've experienced many losses
Fought and beat formidable ills
Now facing these hurtful new adversities
I've no choice but to swallow, this awful bitter pill

Again, Silence is a mighty tool
I'm becoming proficient at its use
I wish things were quite different
But can't accept any behavior, bordering on abuse

I Will Not Let You Break Me
Won't let you bring my spirit down,
Be aware of the cautious demeanor
You'll experience when I'm around

Silence is a mighty tool
I wish I never had to wield
But your actions made it necessary
I don't owe you how I feel

Another Lesson, Another Loss

Another lesson, another loss
Take it as a lesson learned
You've presented all the evidence
And now court has adjourned

No matter the verdict that you wish for
The truth, is just what it is
Despite your honest efforts
He simply doesn't want you, as his

It's another valuable lesson learned
And yet another loss to mourn
But you're stronger, and you're wiser
You'll survive just as you did before

There Is Always Something, Just Out Of View

There is always something, just out of view
Something, someone, didn't want you to see
Cause it's not part of the chosen, painted picture
Truth is not at all you thought it would be

If it'd been caught at a different angle
One that better, represented the truth
And although you display quite a different image
Actual encounters, found you aloof

Billions, hell trillions, are earned, and spent, each year
On having the option of hiding whatever your truth is
We live in the time and space of social media
Seeking external approval, is how we live
Stop concerning yourself with what others think
About how you're living, or what you drive
Take some pride in your integrity and loyalty
Know what you've got, comes from deep inside

Too often there's some fact, that's kept just out of view
Something, someone, didn't want others to know
Instead hone in on what you're best at
And let your true, unique, personality show

Let Go

Let go and let God, they're all telling me
That's most often the advice, that people will give
And that worryin' ain't gon' fix nothin
Guess the facts are, It is, just what it is

Sometimes you really just can't do nothin
No matter how much you'd really like to
You find your hands, have been tied tightly
No time for fixing others, while busy fixing, You

Ask yourself a couple of questions
Have you done your absolute and very best?
Has, absolute and very best been reciprocated?
Honest with yourself answers, will help resolve this mess

Let go and let God, they're all telling me
That's most often the advice, that people will give
And that worryin' ain't gon' fix nothin
Guess the facts are, It is, what it is

Are you hanging in there, cause you gotta?
Or are you Soldiering, strictly out of love
With help from God and true commitment
You'll find comfort and courage from above

Anything worth having just ain't easy
We work for what we value in our lives
We work at being good people, children, parents
Siblings, friends, husbands, and wives

Let go and let God, they're all telling me
That's most often the advice, that people will give
And that worryin' ain't gon' fix nothin
Guess the facts are, It is, what it is

Bored In The House

I'm sad for those who are bored in the house
Cause that's already where you lived
Which means that your home was boring
Before you were forced to shelter in

Can't relate to everyone's boredom
There's so much you always wanted to do
Is it me? Please explain what I'm missing.
Now's your chance, Get 'er done!, I'm confused

Take a photo album trip down memory lane
Waaaay back, when you were just a child
Now remember your favorite bedtime story
Betcha ain't thought bout that in awhile

This time together is rare and it's precious
Our response will determine our future paths
What will your children reminisce and remember?
Their own boredom, or memories made to last

Imagination will cure your boredom
I can't even begin to make a list
This is the time you always hoped for
The Viral Genie has granted your wish

Home, they say is where the heart is
Are you truly bored at home? Is it true?
Or did you just want to be Tik Tok famous
And being home with loved ones is ok with you

Happy, Happy, Merry Day

Happy, Happy, Merry Day
There's always something to celebrate
Before you're done with the last one,
There's always another occasion on its way

Great News! Congratulations!
We always know the right thing to say.
Are the well wishes given with sincerity?
Or are they empty, and cliché?

My Condolences, Sorry for your loss
Is there anything that I can do?
The hand? Extended with momentary good intent
But are the offers, redeemable and true?

There's always an occasion
Something more to celebrate
Sweet 16th, Golden 50th Year
I'll mark the calendar. When do you graduate?

Spend quality time with each other
For we know not, the day or time
Show each other the love you feel
Before either has to say goodbye

Share the simple moments
No labeled day required
Find beauty in each new day we get
No candy, flowers, or declarations desired

Happy, Happy, Merry Day
Find in each day a reason to smile
If for nothing more than the peaceful look
On the face of your sleeping child

So Much Advice

So much advice is being offered
Bout shit I've "already done"
When I sought advice "before" my actions
"Suggestions or direction"? I found none

But now "All" could have done it better
Offering opinions on how to "improve"
Then as I look harder at my, "advisor"?
Yo Man, Yo shit don't even work for you

Now I don't wanna, appear at all ungrateful
I'm well aware, I've been at times, "in need"
But I no longer seek your approval
For the much I've survived, and learned indeed

"I Will" succeed, cause, God? He got me!
And I'll keep striving to do His Will
Thanks, but I'll do what "I" wanna
I hear what you're saying, But not for real

"So Much" advice is being offered
Bout shit I've "already done"
When I sought advice "before" my actions
"Suggestions or direction"? I found none

Melting Pot

You say my home can't be a melting pot
Where ALL who come could add flavor
Cause now we refuse new ingredients
We don't want a soup to savor

We once took pride in our mesh of heritages
We've forgotten what makes good soup
We separate like oil and water
Forming flava disturbing groups

Insanity, by very definition
Is repeating the same damned thing
And expecting something different
Than the "insane behavior" it's gonna bring

My house will remain a melting pot
Where ALL who come can add flavor
Where we practice love and tolerance
And look out for friends, family, and neighbors

Sorry Mr. Springer

Baby pics?, Sorry not enough.
"He" and his twin sister look just the same
We're in an age of technology
We can choose to play many games

Whose fault is it ladies anyway
That a woman's look is easily dittoed by some dude
WE have created the perception
That beauty is a wig, lashes, and big ole' boobs

So, if you're worried that he's on the down low
Or that "she" may have been born a man
Take 1, 2, 3, or even more steps backwards
Before you take, "That there one" to bed

Baby pics? Sorry not enough y'all
I need DNA and polygraphs
And if my questions piss you off?
At which of us do you think I'd rather be mad?

Tune Out Game

My tune out games is on point y'all
And it's getting tighter everyday
If your words are not the truth
Why am I listening anyway?

There's someone always talking
Wanting to express their point of view
But are their words at all useful?
Is their course, what's right for you?

Conversations are continuously happening
You can't know the details of but a few
Can't make your decisions based on
What others will think of you

Get your tune out game on point y'all
And consistently tighten it everyday
If what you're hearing ain't the truth?
Why are you listening anyway...?

Ali

The good book needs another chapter
Fittingly named…. Ali
For he bore resemblance to a second coming
He came to teach us strength and peace

He lived his life with purpose
Taught his children to do the same
He practiced peaceful living
Yet for years they scoffed at his very name

He stood for truth and fought for justice
Raised his children with unconditional love
He had a higher calling
He was reppin' the man above

No matter how profound his words were
He was often speaking into a void
He recorded when no one was listening
He was not to be ignored

He professed "I am The Greatest"
And lived his life as such
And from all that hear his chosen name
The respect he commands is MUCH

If he had been the second coming
We would have missed the message yet again
We failed to see the glory
That lived deep within the man

Bottom Of The Totem Pole

Bottom of the totem pole
Strugglin' to be seen
You, can't fully understand
Just what it's like, to be me

Always behind the eight ball
I'm viewed with much suspicion
Never with respect and equality
Both seem, just words for wishin'

Waking early every morning
Working hard just to be free
With all the unfair obstacles
It's exhausting to be me

One day I'll get a fair shake
To stand on my merit alone
To be viewed with all the others
Upon this totem pole

Butch

Let me tell you bout a special man
Those that know him understand
Butch was quite the legend
Butch, was quite a man

He proudly served his country
Lived life uplifting his fellow man
Was a father to his children
And was truly a standup friend

He was also a fierce competitor
You betta bring it all, on the court, or field
The Art of Defense was his superpower
The war sports stories you've heard, are real

Life unfolded and he made decisions
One, leaving the block, joining the USMC
Then later returning and becoming a fireman
And as time marched on he became OG

He will never be forgotten
So many lives did he touch
All that knew and loved him
We all miss him very much

We miss your distinct unique personality
Strong, loud, and oft times brash (LOL)
But if you ever found yourself in need
There wasn't a better friend to have

Had to share with your bout this special man
Those that know him? Y'all understand
Butch was quite the legend
Butch, was quite a man

Why Not?

Why Not? Who Says? Why Can't I?
I decide life goals each day
How bad do I really want it?
Am I, Walkin', or Talkin', Hustle Game?

Humble, in my many talents
I've no need for accolades
Satisfactions comes in the harvest
And firm foundations I have lain

Why Not? Who Says? Why can't I?
No reason I can't be my very best
Self-confidence, determination, and crazy work ethic
Sets me apart from all the rest

Quiet are my victories
No need to brag or boast
Reward comes in the benefits
And successful defensive riposte

Why Not? Who Says? Why can't I?
Won't let adversity halt my grind
If I want it?, I'mma put the work in and do it
Success and efforts, are intertwined

Survivor

I've survived, and then survived again
Much harder things than this
I also take some comfort in knowing
One day, I will be missed

I'm hardened and hurt, but not broken
YOU, can't be the camel's back, breaking straw
This experience too, I will survive, Potna
You're a vicious lesson learned, That's All.

So, call it what you wanna
What was asked, was what was fair
Won't take blame for your behavior
What you lost, was loving and rare

I'm hardened, and hurt, but not broken
YOU, won't be, the camel's back, breaking straw
This experience too, I will survive, Potna
You're a vicious lesson learned, That's All.

Shocking Discoveries

New shocking discoveries everyday
Things I would have never believed to be true
Shocked at newly realized realities
The learned truth, is not what I thought of you

I loved, respected and trusted
That I was loved, as true as I gave
But when the chips were down below sea level
With love? Was far from how you behaved

New shocking discoveries everyday
I'll retain the hurtful lessons I have learned
Be aware, our love is damaged forever and always
You are no longer one of my concerns

No need to check in, check on, or check with me
You've insulted the very core of who I am
And if that is really your opinion
All I can think to say is, Damn?

Did more than I've learned, I should have
Certainly, more than many others would
You know I would've simply done anything asked
Yet you question if my intentions are good

New shocking discoveries everyday
Won't let them harden the very core of me
But I ain't nobody's damn fool either
Where I always was? There for you? Is no longer
where I'll be

New shocking discoveries everyday
I will always do and give my best
And reciprocal loyalty and honesty is a must
I can not, will not, accept anything less

End Game

So focused on the end game
Not taking time to enjoy the journey
Missing knowing the smell of flowers
Or laughter when things are funny

So determined to be successful
Missing life as you claw to the top
Not noticing your kid is being bullied
Until his bully-er, has been fatally shot

So focused on your end game
Missing life as you go along
Creating the very circumstance
That facilitate things going wrong

Can we please change our focus?
Get our F**king priorities straight
Please let us change our behavior
Before once again, we cared too late

Ashamed

I am ashamed of my behavior...
Ashamed of some things I've said
I speak too often from emotion
Without stopping to use my head

I am ashamed of my harsh judgements
We all have a story and a past
We may understand another's burden
If we would only care to ask

I am ashamed of mankind's behavior
Whether tadpole or the garden your believed start
Ashamed of mankind's progression
His core, his empathy, his heart

Distrust and deceit among men began early
Lies, shame, envy and murder too
When you venture through mans history
What do you expect modern man to do?

I am ashamed for all I've done wrong
For ever uttering a divisive word
Ashamed for not always standing up
Against all negative words I've heard

I'm most ashamed of really believing
That mankind is eternally lost
When I know we are resilient,
And will bounce back at all costs

One day we'll learn the lesson
That shame and regret will teach
We must be ashamed and change behavior
To reach potential greatness, all of the, You's and Me's

Thanks For Letting Me Be Part Of Your Struggle

Thanks for letting me be part of your struggle
It's a privilege to be part of your life
I pray my actions are helpful
And bring relief in times of strife

I know you're very guarded
Not quick to let folks in
Let me show you true loyalty
Loving you through thick and thin

You have your loyal, "second"
In your "honor" challenges and duels
Anticipating your every want and need
I will always be there for you

I'm here to ease your struggle
It's a privileged to be in your life
I hope I can be helpful
And bring comfort in times of strife

Tell me

Tell me, Tell me, Who's my daddy?
Tell me, what's his name?
Tell me, tell me who he is?
And do we look the same

Tell me, Tell me who's my dad
Tell me where he's been
Tell me, Tell me where's MY father
Will he want to be my friend?

Did you ever love him?
Or was he just a fling
Was I conceived by passionate hearts?
Or was he, just one of those things

Tell me, Tell me, I'll ask again
You seem to be avoiding the question
Tell me, Tell me, I'm growing up
I wanna know my heritage

I'm trying to chart my future
Without knowing much of my past
Please don't make me suffer
'Cause y'all were young and you're still mad

It's kinda not your decision

I have a right to know
It's your job to tell me
Let all that anger go

I simply wanna know him
I wanna see him face to face
I wanna learn to love him
It's not your decision to make

Tell me, Tell me who's genes I carry
Again, I ask for the truth
Don't take from me in my adulthood
What you've stolen from my youth

Tell me, Tell me, before you're gone
Don't take this secret to the grave
You hide him away with your memories
Like he was the worst mistake you've made

Mother is very ill now,
We don't know from day to day
Thank God she broke her silence
Just before she passed away

This Is My Square

I've already claimed this square Potna
You gotta go claim one of your own
I've got all that's necessary to be happy
Within the confines of my home

I could choose to make a rare addition
Hoping you'll prove to be the one
But if what you say at any time doesn't add up?
That chance will be quickly gone

I've already claimed this square Brotha!
Ain't gonna let no one knock me off of mine
If your thoughts are based on the old me
Understand she's been left far behind

I've emerged a better person
A better sense of what I'm worth
Changing like a caterpillar to a butterfly
Part of the cycle of life on earth

Done long since claimed this square Potna
Joining with my square with one of your own
Both first maintained independently

Then forming the best square ever known

Damn Mama…

Damn Mama, What the hell?
What have you done to me?
You said my dad was Jim or John
Now possible dads? are at least three

DNA results, now they don't lie
Neither Jim nor John are the one
Dear Mama, what else have you lied about
Seems you were wild and having fun

What did you think when you found out
You had slipped up and made a baby
All these years, you were Oh so sure
Never mentioning the other maybes

You harbored hate, then passed it on
You let it fester and affect
Now everything you've ever taught me
I now look at as, suspect

This is no simple matter
It is my heritage, which is at stake
How dare you not know my father

What a hell of a mistake to make

Respect

How far are we gonna take "Fashion"?
What's next? Are we gonna get out here nude?
Then when we notice someone gawking
Cop an attitude and come back rude

Why are fishnet and pasties gracing the red carpet
Mini skirts and stilettos at the PTA
Why are you loudly making phone calls?
Then disbelieving someone had "sumptin" to say

Don't think you'll be respected
The respect you say that you're due
But based on your very behavior
Your, biggest enemy, is YOU

Stop blaming "all/and" the others
Take a good look in that mirror
Face and fix those demons
You'll be better for facing your fears

Restore respectable behavior
The little things mean so much

No son wants his moms skirt so short
That everyone can see her butt

Please let's get back to basics
Let's teach our kids how to live life
How to be respectful to others
And productively face life's strife

Show them self-respect and confidence
Teach them to stand up proud
Conduct themselves respectfully
And opportunities will be abound

What do we think will happen?
If we continue to breed disrespect
Let's teach compassion, empathy, and love
And if we don't, chaos is what we'll get

I Can't Breathe

I CAN'T breathe, That's what George Floyd told them
Yet they remained kneeling on his neck
And his family is now forever broken
Arrest have been made, but justice has not been served yet

I try not to speak hypothetically
Easy to say what i would have done it I had been there
But truth is, watching a man being murdered
I believe is much more than my heart could bare

I CAN'T breathe, that's what a dying man told them
Yet they ignored his cries and calls for help
some have chosen to blame the victim's character
Like this has not, and could not, happened to anyone else

Let us review and remember some of the other murderous policemen's victims
Like Freddie Gray, Sandra Bland, Eric Garner, and young Tamir Rice
In 2018 the world videoed at least 15 unarmed black men murdered by police officers
Yet only 3 of the charged were convicted, we all know that shit aint right

They've been killing us since they stole us
I know this brutality is in no way new
But this shit has become fucking ridiculous
Maybe violence is necessary, for the laws of justice to be reviewed

I CAN'T breathe, is what we are all now saying
Yet they remain kneeling on our necks
Floyds family, along with the rest the world is demanding action
And with global unity, maybe justice is what we will finally get

Zero Motive…

I have zero motive to lie to anyone
Let's first get that understood
I do and say exactly as I please
So, if I did it, assume I decided that I could

So, before you decide to express disagreement regarding my opinion
Like it or not I stand firm on my actions and my words
I have zero motive to lie to anyone brotha
Truth is, my decisions, are not your concern

So, if you're doubting my ass can cash my mouths paycheck
Or if you're confused and/or critical of what the fuck I've said
Remember interpretation usually affords confusion
Just believe the words comin outta my mouth and not that shit, made up in yo head

I'm willing to bet if we have a civil discussion
At minimum, we could agree to disagree
But meanwhile, what you won't do, is question my integrity
Your opinion, doesn't make a liar, of me

Now back to my original proclamation
I have ZERO motive to lie to anyone
There are few whose opinion I concern myself with
And of those few? You, are, simply not, one

So please check yourself, when calling me a liar
Cause shit ain't working out as you had planned
And when you're done with your opinion-based accusations
The truth, will still be the motherfucking truth, in the end

I hope you have enjoyed

"Unapologetic"

As promised, I will also give you a peek into my next book

"Fractured Folks"

And my first book

"Inspired" Lyrical Thoughts of a St Louis Poet

I have also included my small collection of erotic poetry

FOR ADULTS ONLY!!

(Be warned and aware there is adult material, subject matter and language in the final chapter

"Erotic Rhythms"

My 2 Me's

The 2 Me's are always beefin'
Always with a different point of view
One will give you the benefit of the doubt
While the other is surely doubting you

One's full of hope, and energy
A delight to most she meets
The other? She's tough as nails
With caution, is how she greets

The 2 Me's are always beefin'
Always with a different point of view
One will give you the benefit of the doubt
While the other is surely doubting you

When both Me's come together
And find a love or common goal
I am a better, stronger person
Whose future is bright and bold

My 2 Me's must stop the beefin'
Join and move up the learning tree
Meshing the best of each of them
Revealing the very best of Me

Teach One

If your fellowman is failing? Inform him
If he is lacking knowledge? Please teach
If each "One" of us, would teach "One"
Imagine how many "Ones" we could reach

Oppressed has been our economy and opportunity
Inadequate neighborhoods, education, and healthcare
One certainty is, this is… systematic
Break 'em down, Keep 'em down and Leave 'em there

Local roads and bridges, old and failing
No funds for elective programs in our schools
Yet, a few miles down the road and 'round a few corners
Life is lived, by a different set of… privileged rules

Where a young man was excused of vehicular murder, based on… affluenza
And billionaires get a slap on the wrist for buying… little girls
Where a black man was choked and killed by cops for… selling loose cigarettes
What the hell is happening in our world?

If your fellowman is failing? Inform him
If he is lacking knowledge? Please take a moment to teach
Cause if each One of us, would teach One
Just imagine how many "Ones" we could reach

The Love Meant For Me

The love meant for me will be easy
No feelings of deficiency, will it bring
We'll be friends, lovers, and teammates
With devotion, not contingent, on any one particular thing

We'll both know, 'cause God will tell us
And neither of us, will doubt his voice
There'll be no compromise necessary
For true love, to be the choice

The love meant for me will be easy
No convincing or coercing will be required
The depth of the love will be evident
Only sincerity, and honesty will be desired

That love won't have me wondering
What more, there is, I need to do
To ensure that the one that I'm loving
Is also happy, loving me too

Adoptee

They say but you were deliberately loved, Ms. Adoptee
And say I must feel lucky and adored
Because someone *chose* to love me
I must be certainly better off than my before?

But there are simple things many take for granted
Realities and facts I was denied
Like the whos and whats about who made me
I have an eternal search brewing deep inside

I have a great thirst for knowledge of my history
There are answers needed to learn my core
Yet all think that I'm just so lucky
Certainly better off than my before?

They say, Why you askin' all these questions?
Are you sure you wanna learn the truths?
There may be pain in the realities
And not joy when you find the, Whos

Yes, I was deliberately loved and chosen
But first, I was abandoned, not adored
Robbed of all knowledge of the real me
Still think, better off than my before?

I deserve to know my heritage
Do I look more like him or her
You have robbed me of my identity
I'm not certain even of my date of birth

I am blessed to be deliberately loved
And thankful to be chosen and adored
But don't fool yourself bout how lucky
For I am also forever haunted, by my before

Poems you missed if you haven't read my first book

"Inspired" Lyrical Thoughts of A St Louis Poet

What's the "All"

What's the "All" you're searching for
What is that one dream, that is your fuel
What' feeling makes you happiest
What brings out the very best in you

Be sure what you're seeking, is needed
Be certain the search for answers, hasn't left you blind
Healing is found, not in the search, but in the conversation
Perspective propels you forward, and pushes grief, further behind

What's the "All" that you're striving for
What aspirations inspire you to move
What seeds planted, are you most proud of
What cultivates the very best of you

Have you profited from life's lemons?
Making world famous lemonade
While searching for that elusive silver lining
And praying that God will show the better way

What's the "All" you've prayed for
Is joy and happiness your ultimate goal
Just sit back and marvel at God's blessings
He'll heal the broken pieces and make you whole

One

Fellow occupants of the planet Earth
We are collectively… One
Having faced global, simultaneous danger
A new World Order has begun

Hierarchy, power, wealth, and exclusivity
Have determined the order of the peck
Yet we Thrive, with Collective Purpose
Haven't we figured that fact out yet

The human race is only as strong as
It's failing, weakest, link
If we are to be our "Brothers Keepers"
We must offer knowledge and assistance, without a blink

The world found itself quarantined
Because there was/is danger to its health
We cannot save the masses
Thinking only of ourselves

A new norm is on the horizon
The world will never be quite the same
And for the change to be positive
We must adjust how we behave

Love family, friends, and neighbors
Spread God's love to everyone
Realize collective, responsible behavior
Is how humanity's war will be won

Vessels

I've met, head-on, many challenges
Trudged along quite the muddy road
Told folks I was gonna do better
"Yea right", is what I was told

But here I stand, just as I said
They now congratulate and cheer
Despite the doubting and the wondering
"Here I am", Told ya I'd be right here

Some joyous occasions harbor sadness
Some opportunities lost for good
But if all things happen for some reason
Life must be happening as it should

We don't get to chart our path as a vessel
Vessels through which blessings can flow
One day you'll learn of your loves impact
From someone you knew many moons ago

God's plan? We can only wonder
Some doors will open, and some will close
Forgive yourself, then forgive others
And keep moving with the help of the Lord

You Must Be 18 Years Or Older To Continue Reading

Be Aware

What follows contains Adult material, subject matter and language.

If you choose to continue,

You may find yourself clutching your pearls.

You've been warned…

Enjoy!

Welcome to the final chapter of

"Unapologetic"

Erotic Rhythms

Enjoy

Hood Chick

Hood Chicks? They got that "Good Good"
None you've had before can compare
You only think you've experienced ecstasy
Till hood pussy takes you there

It's warm, wet, and wicked
She'll feed it to you before you slide in
And if she graces you with her head game
Your dick's desire won't ever be the same again

A hood chick, see she's a lil ratchet
Stilettos, long legs, and a mini skirt
Be sure you're ready for good hood pussy
Cause she'll fuck you till it hurts

Hood chicks ain't out here flirting
All that coy shit, just ain't her
If fuckin' is what she's wanting
Then fuckin' is what will occur

If you're lucky, and get some hood pussy
Never again will you be the same
But don't forget, she's hood nigga
She'll dismiss you as quickly as you came

Hood Chicks? They got that "Good Good"
None you've had can compare
If you want to experience pure ecstasy
Try a hood chick, if you dare

Wet Words Wednesday

When I heard about Wet Words Wednesday
I decided to write a new, but nasty poem
And although it was a new genre for me
I had to be sure, to set a fire in your loins

I said, hmm let me think, I'll paint an erotic picture
One from which they won't want to escape
Leaving them aching, moist, hard and horny
One to put all on the same freaky, dirty page

Now close your eyes and feel the firm, yet soft kisses
Being placed first upon the nape of your neck
Now feel the tongue and hands as they start a roamin'
Ladies, the thought, I know, has your panties wet

Now, for you guys, lend me your ear, come listen
As your manhood is poetically devoured
Feel the well-placed sex-filled word-kisses
A symphony of ecstasy lasting for hours

Now that I have you both ripe and ready
Ready for Simon to say, you can unload
With an undulating melody of words and syllables
Simon Says, let loose, relax, and explode

I wanted to be sure to paint a picture
Make you imagine awaiting asses in the air
Evoking thoughts of being an anxious participant
Doing things you previously wouldn't dare

I hope you've enjoyed my ode to Wet Word Wednesdays
I hope I've ignited all the listening loins
And new genre, but I'll write others
So, I'll be back with another wet poem

BDC

If I had a big dick, Nigga !!
Wouldn't be a woman safe for miles
Women would be out there googling my dick potna
Chasing My swag, my flow, my style

Then once she was simply captivated
I'd let her explore my big ass dick
First with her lovely fingers
Then she would lick and suck it for a bit

Then maybe I would introduce her to my tongue, it's oh so talented
Lick her like she was dripping, melting ice cream
I'd thrust my tongue repeatedly inside her wetness
Talents to make her mind and her body scream

If I had a big dick, Oh my goodness
It would stay wet and warm and hard
I would be a nasty, sensual, considerate lover
Blissful, multiple orgasms would be her certain reward

With every deeper stroke I would please her
As I gazed lustfully into her beautiful eyes
And Daddy is what she would call me
As I turn her over and hit it passionately from behind

Good Lawd If I had a big dick Nigga
Whew frfr I probably wouldn't be shit
Cause I would spend my whole life fucking
Making use of my big ole dick

I'd probably become an entrepreneur
Just call 1-800 come get this dick
I'd Have the ladies asking Alexa and Siri
How to find me, so I can swell that clit

Again, If I had a big dick Nigga
There wouldn't be a pussy dry for miles
Cause they be wet with wonder while they're googling my dick potna
Chasin' my Swag, my Flow, my Style

Stranger Danger

I'm convinced there's a conspiracy
I mean the lighting in the club
I took home a beautiful woman named Belinda
And woke up with a dude named Bud

I must, step back and reevaluate
Stop having encounters with total strangers
Cause each time that it happens
The aftermath is praying away the danger

Lawd, hope she don't have something
Especially something that can't be cured
Then mid prayer you stop and think
Déjà vu, I've done this dumb shit before

I'm convinced there's a conspiracy
I mean the lighting in the club
I took home a beautiful woman named Belinda
And woke up with a dude named Bud

Made in the USA
Monee, IL
29 June 2024